THE *BIG* PICTURE
MEN
WHO CHANGED THE WORLD

BY GRACE JONES

THE SECRET BOOK COMPANY

©2018
The Secret Book Company
King's Lynn
Norfolk PE30 4LS

ISBN: 978-1-912171-84-2

Written by:
Grace Jones

Edited by:
Kirsty Holmes

Designed by:
Matt Rumbelow

A catalogue record for this book
is available from the British Library.

Images are courtesy of Shutterstock.com. With thanks to Getty Images, Thinkstock Photo and iStockphoto. 1/2 – Nestor Rizhniak, Pressmaster, Everett Collection, Alessia Pierdomenico, Kiselev Andrey Valerevich, Pemaphoto, noche, Pressmaster. 4/5 – Pressmaster, Everett Collection, Alessia Pierdomenico, Kiselev Andrey Valerevich, Pemaphoto, noche. 6/7 – catwalker, Everett Historical, M DOGAN, howcolour. 8/9 – Georgios Kollidas, fad82, Jan Martin Will, Michelangelus, RaulAlmu, Elena Medvedeva, Venomous Vector, MatiasDelCarmine, PPVector, 10/11 – Alessia Pierdomenico, Naeblys, SAPhotog, Thomas Pajot, Radu Bercan, davooda 14/15 – Georgios Kollidas, glo, Oleg Golovnev, Everett Historical, Jakub Krechowicz, HildaWeges Photography, filborg. 16/17 – Evan El-Amin, FabrikaSimf, Chris Parypa Photography, Heidi Besen, Evan El-Amin, Cube29. 18/19 – Scott Woodham Photography, Vladitto, Featureflash Photo Agency, Artur. B. 20/21 – city100, MarkoV87, Rajagopal S, davooda, Malikzade. 22 – drserg, Diego Cervo, guteksk7, 24Novembers, vectorfusionart, MaraZe, tulpahn, igorstevanovic, Khakimullin Aleksandr, Rashad Ashurov, PureSolution, Sentavio. 24 – Stocksnapper, JasaShmasa, Igor Bulgarin, India Picture. 26/27 – Stocksnapper, JasaShmasa, Igor Bulgarin, India Picture. 28/29 – Everett Historical, Georgios Kollida.

All facts, statistics, web addresses and URLs in this book were verified as valid and accurate at time of writing. No responsibility for any changes to external websites or references can be accepted by either the author or publisher.

CONTENTS

Page 4   Men Who Changed the World

Page 6   Martin Luther King

Page 8   Sir Isaac Newton

Page 10   Nelson Mandela

Page 12   Benjamin Franklin

Page 14   Leonardo Da Vinci

Page 16   Barack Obama

Page 18   Muhammad Ali

Page 20   Albert Einstein

Page 22   Sir Tim Berners-Lee

Page 24   William Shakespeare

Page 26   Mahatma Gandhi

Page 28   Timeline: Men Who Changed the World

Page 30   Glossary

Page 32   Index

Words that look like **this** can be found in the glossary on page 30.

MEN WHO CHANGED THE WORLD

Over thousands of years, men have achieved many extraordinary **feats**, from making ground-breaking discoveries to dreaming up mind-boggling inventions and fighting for what they believed in.

Many men have achieved great things that have changed the world forever. In this book, you'll learn about some of the most inspiring men who have allowed us to do things such as use the Internet, live in a more equal world and even use electricity.

Scientist

Politician

Leader

Inventor

How did Martin Luther King change civil rights?

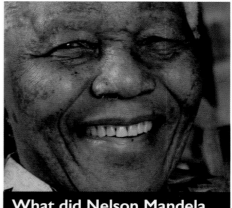

When did Sir Isaac Newton discover gravity?

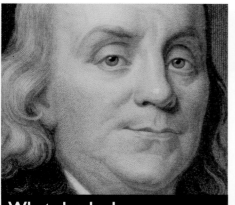

What did Nelson Mandela do for South Africa?

What shocked Benjamin Franklin?

How did Leonardo da Vinci influence art?

Why was Barack Obama a very special president?

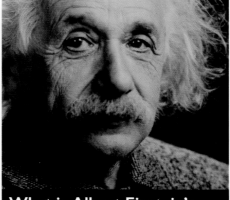

Was Muhammad Ali the best sportsman ever?

What is Albert Einstein's Special Theory of Relativity?

How did Tim Berners-Lee get us all online?

How did Shakespeare's plays change the world?

Who was Mahatma Gandhi and what did he do for India?

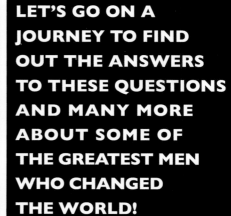

LET'S GO ON A JOURNEY TO FIND OUT THE ANSWERS TO THESE QUESTIONS AND MANY MORE ABOUT SOME OF THE GREATEST MEN WHO CHANGED THE WORLD!

MARTIN LUTHER KING

In 1950s America, black people were **discriminated** against in all parts of life. **Segregation** laws meant that black Americans were not allowed to go to the same places that white Americans could. Even if they could they had to sit in different areas or rooms away from the white people.

In 1955, a woman named Rosa Parks refused to give up her seat on the bus for a white passenger in Montgomery, USA. She was arrested for breaking the segregation laws. A **civil rights activist** called Martin Luther King heard about this and organised a **boycott** of the buses in Montgomery, which lasted for 381 days. It was so successful that segregation on buses came to end.

Schools, restaurants and toilets are just some of the places where black people were segregated from white people.

Rosa Parks and the Montgomery bus boycott started a wave of protests across America that are considered to have started the **Civil Rights Movement**. The Civil Rights Movement fought for **racial equality** and an end to segregation.

After the Montgomery bus boycott, King became one of the main leaders of the Civil Rights Movement. He fought for racial equality in all areas of society using peaceful protest rather than violence. In 1963, Martin Luther King helped to organise a huge march on Washington. Over 250,000 people attended to fight for their civil rights.

In 1964 the Civil Rights Act was passed, which ended segregation in public schools, stopped discrimination at work and gave African-Americans protection from police violence. Martin Luther King is remembered as one of the main leaders of the Civil Rights Movement. Even today, his actions and words inspire others around the world with his message of hope and peace.

"I have a dream that my four little children will one day live in a nation where they will not be judged by the colour of their skin, but by the content of their character."

In 1968, Martin Luther King was shot and killed. Over 100,000 people attended his funeral procession.

7

SIR ISAAC NEWTON

Sir Isaac Newton was a scientist, mathematician and **astronomer**, and is considered to be one of the most important scientists in the history of the world. Even though Newton discovered many things, one of his most famous discoveries was gravity.

Newton was known for having a bad temper and arguing with other scientists.

One day, Newton was sitting beneath an apple tree when an apple fell to the ground. Newton thought about this and wondered why it did not fall sideways or upwards, but why things always fell towards the ground. He worked very hard to try to find the answer to this question and eventually explained it using his theory of gravity.

Newton's theory explained that gravity is a force that attracts two things towards each other. That force, called gravitational pull, must have been what caused the apple to fall to the ground. The more **mass** an object has, the stronger its gravitational force or pull. Because the Earth has a much larger mass than the apple, the Earth's gravitational pull drew the apple to the ground.

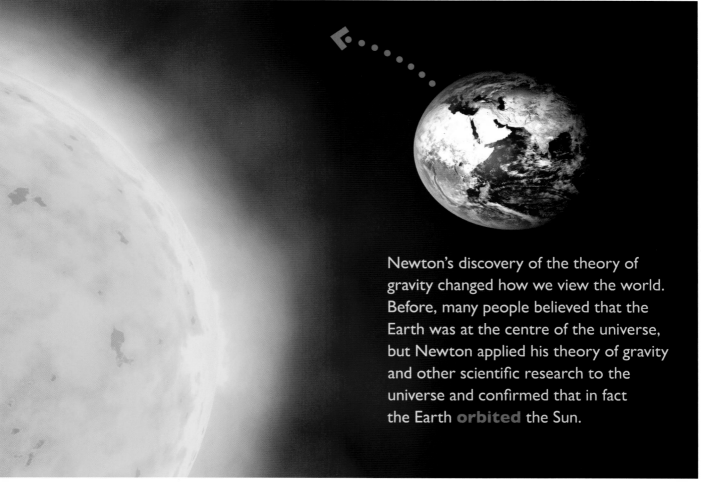

Newton's discovery of the theory of gravity changed how we view the world. Before, many people believed that the Earth was at the centre of the universe, but Newton applied his theory of gravity and other scientific research to the universe and confirmed that in fact the Earth **orbited** the Sun.

Newton also developed a new type of mathematics called calculus and made a reflecting telescope, amongst many other things.

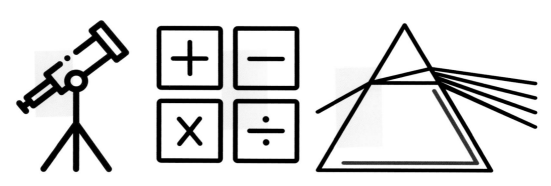

NELSON MANDELA

In 1948, in South Africa, **apartheid laws** were passed. The apartheid laws meant that black people were discriminated against in all parts of life. For example, black people couldn't live in the same areas, do the same jobs or go to the same schools as white people.

FOR USE BY WHITE PERSONS

THESE PUBLIC PREMISES AND THE AMENITIES THEREOF HAVE BEEN RESERVED FOR THE EXCLUSIVE USE OF WHITE PERSONS.

By Order Provincial Secretary

VIR GEBRUIK DEUR BLANKE

HIERDIE OPENBARE PERSEEL EN DIE GERIE DAARVAN IS VIR DIE UITSLUITLIKE GEBRI VAN BLANKES AANGEWYS.

Op Las Provinsiale Sekretar

Nelson Mandela was born in 1918 in Transkei, South Africa. When he was older, he thought apartheid was unfair so he became a civil rights activist in the anti-apartheid movement. He eventually joined the **African National Congress** party (ANC) and became very involved in the fight to end apartheid. In 1962, the South African **government** arrested him and he spent the next 27 years in prison.

In prison he was treated very badly and forced to work very hard every day. However, he never gave up on his dream to end apartheid. In 1990 he was eventually released from prison. After this, apartheid laws were slowly **abolished**. In 1992, all people were given the right to vote. In 1994, the first **democratic** elections were held. The ANC won over 60% of the votes and Nelson Mandela became the president of South Africa.

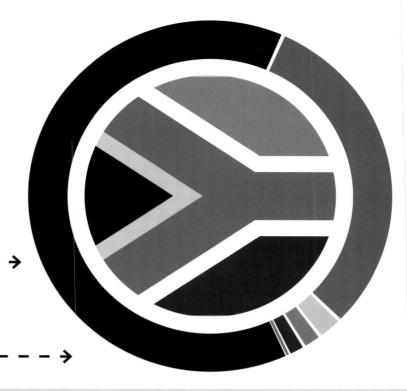

African National Congress   Freedom Front
The National Party   Democratic Party
Inkatha Freedom Party   Other parties

Nelson Mandela fought throughout his life against injustice and inequality. He brought around change that ended apartheid and brought democracy to South Africa and freedom to its people. Nelson Mandela was such an important leader that when he died in 2013, important world leaders from all over the world came to **commemorate** his life and achievements.

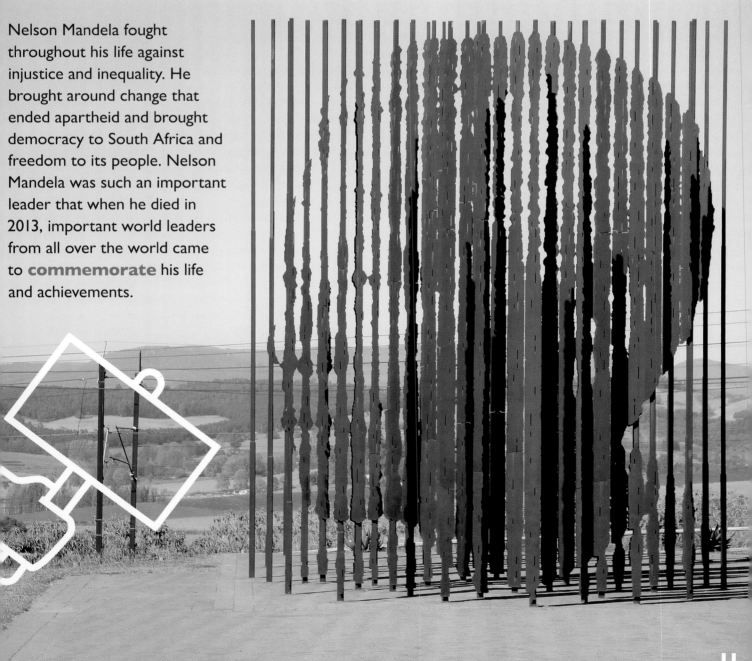

BENJAMIN FRANKLIN

Benjamin Franklin was a scientist who is considered to be the first person to discover how to use electricity. Franklin's discovery has changed the lives of everyone on the planet. It's the reason why we have things such as electric lights instead of candles, and can watch television and use our mobile phones.

Before Franklin's discovery, he believed that electricity could flow between two points. He thought that lightning was one example of his theory and so in 1752 he conducted an experiment to prove it.

When one object is rubbed against another, electricity can be created. Believe it or not, this is not a magic trick; it is just **static electricity** at work.

12

In order to show that lightning was electricity, Franklin flew a kite during a thunderstorm. He tied an iron key to the bottom of the kite string and an iron rod to the top of the kite.

Electricity from the clouds flowed into the iron rod, down the kite string and to the key that he was holding. Because metal is a **conductor** of electricity, this gave him an electric shock and proved his theory to be correct. Luckily, Franklin's kite wasn't hit by lightning as this amount of electricity would have killed him! It is very dangerous to experiment with electricity.

Franklin went on to invent lots more things during his lifetime, including a type of glasses called bifocals and a glass harmonica. He also made many other discoveries about electricity, weather, cooling and light.

Did you know that Franklin was one of the founding fathers who founded North America and made the American Declaration of Independence in 1776?

LEONARDO DA VINCI

Leonardo da Vinci was born in 1452 in Vinci, Italy. From an early age, Leonardo showed he was very good at art and at the age of 14 he began to work under the famous artist Andrea del Verrocchio in Florence. Here he learnt a wide range of skills including painting, sculpting, drawing and even **carpentry**.

At just 20 years old, da Vinci gained a place as a master artist in Florence's Guild Saint Luke and formed his own workshop.

Although not many of da Vinci's original drawings, paintings and sculptures are still around, he is still considered to be one of the greatest artists to have ever lived. One of the most famous paintings in the world, the Mona Lisa, was painted by da Vinci. The picture is now housed in the Louvre museum in Paris and receives over six million visitors every year. Experts estimate that it is now worth over 700 million pounds.

Da Vinci painted in the Renaissance style. The Renaissance period was a time of discovery, observation and a focus on revealing truth.

In 1482, da Vinci was offered a job with the Duke of Milan, Ludovico Sforza. Da Vinci worked for Sforza as a painter, sculptor and even as an inventor too. He would invent and sketch war machines for the Duke. He also designed very early versions of the bicycle, helicopter and aeroplane, but it wasn't until hundreds of years later that his genius was recognised.

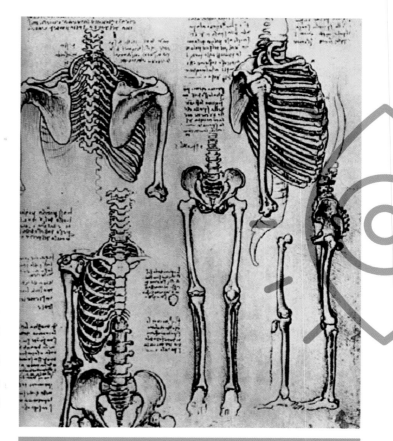

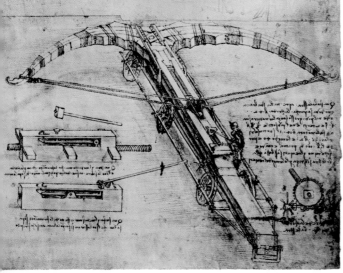

Da Vinci was very interested in the science of the body and made many sketches of body parts.

Leonardo da Vinci was one of the greatest artists in history. He inspired many artists when he lived and he continues to inspire people all over the world today. He is not just a great artist, but he is also recognised as a great inventor and scientist too.

BARACK OBAMA

Barack Obama was born in Hawaii in 1961 to a Kenyan father and an American mother. Obama was intelligent and worked hard at school. After finishing college, he moved to Chicago, USA, to help the communities who lived there. He eventually gained a place at law school, at a very good university called Harvard University.

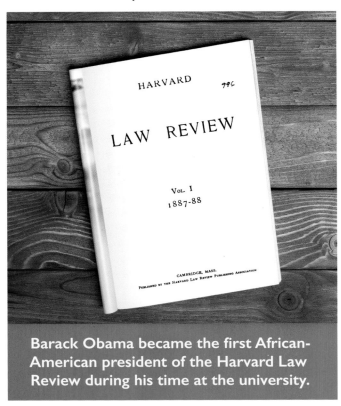

Barack Obama became the first African-American president of the Harvard Law Review during his time at the university.

After he graduated from law school, Obama spent some time teaching law in Chicago. He also joined the Democratic Party, which is a political party in the US. In 2004 he was elected to the US senate. In 2008, he ran to be president of the United States and won the most votes. On the 20th January 2009, Barack Obama officially became the first ever black president of the United States.

The main things that the Democratic Party believes in are equality, human rights, freedom, peace and justice.

During Obama's eight years as president, he achieved many great things that changed American society, the **economy** and America's relationship with the rest of the world. He passed Obamacare, which was a set of laws that gave **medical insurance** to many people who could not previously afford it. He also is considered to have turned a failing economy into a successful one.

Obama started the process of withdrawing all soldiers from Afghanistan and Iraq where they had been fighting wars for a number of years.

Apart from being the first ever black US president, Obama is remembered as a likeable and hard-working president who changed America for the better. He did much for peace, equality and the economy that has changed America forever.

MUHAMMAD ALI

In 1942, Cassius Marcellus Clay, Jr. was born in Kentucky, USA. When he was 12 years old, somebody stole his bike. He was so angry that he set off to fight the person who stole it. But a police officer caught up with him and offered to teach him how to fight. He began to take boxing lessons regularly. He learnt quickly and became very skilled.

When Cassius was growing up, life was difficult because he was a black American. At that time black Americans did not have access to the same opportunities as white Americans.

"I am the greatest! I am the greatest! I'm the king of the world!"

He began fighting with other amateur boxers and won 100 out of 105 fights. In 1960, he travelled to Rome in Italy to fight in the Olympics. He won the gold medal and, when he returned home at the age of 18, he decided to dedicate himself to professional boxing. He also converted to Islam and changed his name to Muhammad Ali. Ali fought in 61 professional boxing matches and won 56 of them.

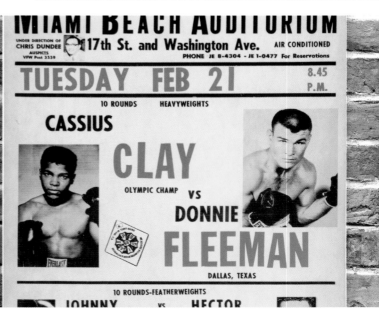

MIAMI BEACH AUDITORIUM

UNDER DIRECTION OF
CHRIS DUNDEE
AUSPICES
VFW Post 3559
17th St. and Washington Ave. AIR CONDITIONED

PHONE JE 8-4304 - JE 1-0477 For Reservations

TUESDAY FEB 21 8.45 P.M.

10 ROUNDS HEAVYWEIGHTS

CASSIUS CLAY
OLYMPIC CHAMP VS DONNIE FLEEMAN
DALLAS, TEXAS

10 ROUNDS-FEATHERWEIGHTS

JOHNNY VS HECTOR

Ali's boxing style was quick and skilful. Despite his weight and size, many would call him a 'ballerina' in the boxing ring because of the way he moved and danced around his opponents and avoided their punches. He also had incredible speed and fitness and could go on fighting for many rounds, unlike lots of his opponents.

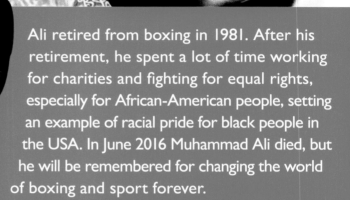

Ali retired from boxing in 1981. After his retirement, he spent a lot of time working for charities and fighting for equal rights, especially for African-American people, setting an example of racial pride for black people in the USA. In June 2016 Muhammad Ali died, but he will be remembered for changing the world of boxing and sport forever.

In 2005, Ali was awarded the Presidential Medal of Freedom from the US president to recognise his work with charities.

#1
Voted the number 1 heavyweight boxer of the 20th century.

1964
Became heavyweight champion of the world in 1964.

56/61
Won 56 out of 61 professional boxing matches.

ALBERT EINSTEIN

Albert Einstein was born in 1879 in Ulm, Germany. From a young age, Einstein was interested in science and maths at school and at home. When he was older he began to study for a degree in physics at university in Zurich, Switzerland. Once finished, he began to work in an office, but continued to study.

UNIVERSITÄT ZÜRICH ZENTRUM

Einstein's experiments were very important. He had many theories about they way light and time actually work. For example, his theories of relativity showed how the speed of light is fixed, but space and time are not fixed – they can bend! He also showed that space and time are part of the same thing and he called this 'spacetime'.

With such an amazing mind, Einstein quickly became a famous scientist and worked on lots of important ideas, mostly about things like light and gravity. Einstein was a Jewish man, and in 1933 when the Nazi party were in power in Germany, he left Europe and went to live and work in America, and went on to win a Nobel Prize for Physics. His most famous formula was E=mc2, which is very complicated but basically means that mass (the amount of something) can be turned into energy, and that even something very small, like an **atom**, can make a huge amount of energy!

This formula is very famous.

Albert Einstein is considered to be one of the most important scientists in the history of the world. He made many discoveries in his lifetime including his special theory of relativity; he proved the existence of the atom and changed the way in which scientists viewed the world. He also influenced many future discoveries and inventions. Televisions and computers are just some of the things that we might not have without Einstein's work.

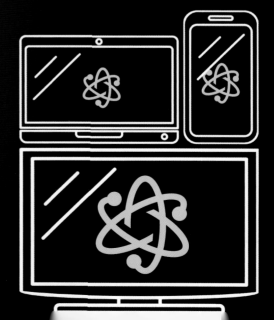

SIR TIM BERNERS-LEE

The Internet seems so essential to our daily lives that it seems like it has been around forever. However, it hasn't been around for as long as you think. The World Wide Web was officially invented in 1989. That's over 20 years ago and, in history terms, that's a very short amount of time.

Tim Berners-Lee was working for a company when his earliest ideas of the Internet were formed. He found it frustrating that he had to get different information on different computers, each using a different programme that he had to learn. He had an idea to create one system on which all people could access all information at all times. Berners-Lee turned his idea into a reality and created the World Wide Web.

Berners-Lee created an information space where people could access and share documents, images, videos and audio files. This **virtual** space, the Internet, has allowed people to communicate much more easily with one another and access huge amounts of information. Nowadays we can use the Internet to do practically everything – to order food, buy clothes and even help us to do our homework!

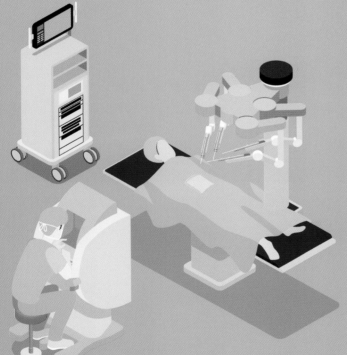

The Internet has given people access to an enormous amount of human knowledge. This has enabled people to learn and develop many new technologies such as instant messaging, video calling and even a robot that can help a surgeon to perform an operation on a person from really far away! The Internet is an important invention because it has connected us all.

Although Berners-Lee is considered to be the first person to invent the Internet, much of the technology he used to do so had already been invented by other people.

WILLIAM SHAKESPEARE

William Shakespeare was born in 1564 in Stratford-Upon-Avon in England. His father, also called William, was a business owner, and his mother, Mary, was the daughter of a landowner. When the younger William was 18, he married a woman called Anne Hathaway who he went on to have three children with. After his marriage Shakespeare moved to London to write and act in plays.

Not much is known about Shakespeare's education, but it is likely his parents were able to pay for him to have a good education.

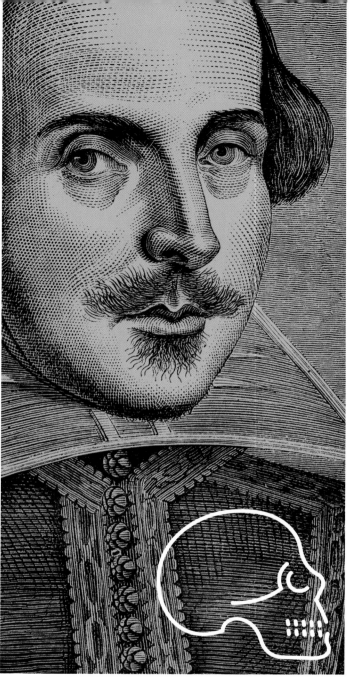

When in London, Shakespeare worked as an actor for a company called the Lord Chamberlain's Men. He also wrote plays for the company that were popular and interesting to many people at the time. His early plays were mainly comedies such as Much Ado About Nothing, or plays that focussed on certain parts of history, such as Henry V.

Shakespeare also wrote many poems in his lifetime and has published 150 sonnets. Many of them are still very famous today.

When the company's theatre was shut down, they **dismantled** the building and moved it across the River Thames to rebuild it at another spot. They called the new theatre the Globe Theatre. The theatre could hold 3,000 people. The plays became very popular and were usually full for every performance. During this time Shakespeare is considered to have written his greatest plays.

The stage was specially designed to include a ceiling, columns and walls. Musicians were trained to produce special effects and noises during performances to make them more lifelike.

All the World's a Stage

Shakespeare died in 1616, but his **legacy** will live on forever. He is considered to be the greatest and most influential playwright in history. His influence was so great that many pupils still study his work in schools and universities all over the world and his plays continue to be made into films and performed in theatres worldwide.

Shakespeare is said to have written 38 plays in his lifetime.

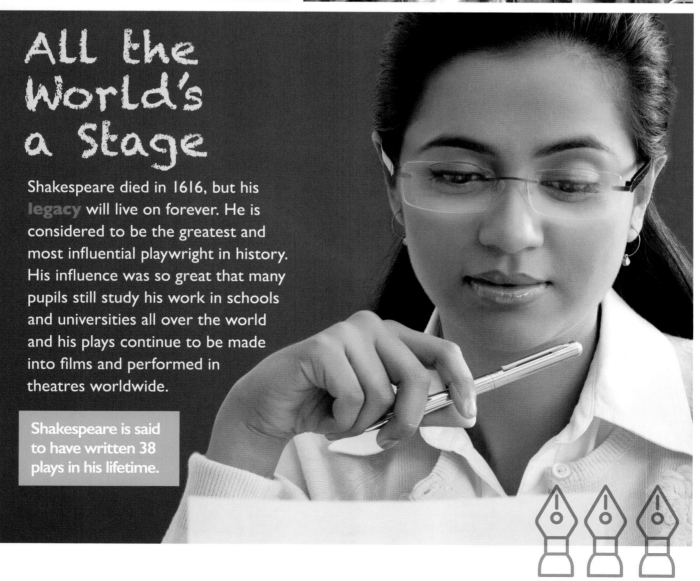

MAHATMA GANDHI

Mohandas Karamchand Gandhi was born in 1948 in New Delhi, India to a rich family. When he was 19 years old, he moved to England to study law at University College London. He returned to India after he finished studying and started a law company. The company wasn't successful so he took a job as a lawyer in South Africa. Here, he experienced racial discrimination.

People call him 'Mahatma' rather than his real name Mohandas. This is a title that is only used for a sacred person or one who has very special powers.

Once he returned home, his experiences in South Africa encouraged him to become a civil rights activist in India. At the time, India was part of the **British Empire**. This meant that Britain owned and controlled India and its people. Many people in India wanted independence from British rule.

Gandhi organised non-violent protests against British rule. These were acts of **civil disobedience** and included things like refusing to work. Gandhi was arrested and put in prison many times during this period because the British were scared of how powerful he was.

So many thousands of people were involved in Gandhi's protests, they started to become a big problem for the British government.

In 1930, when Britain raised the price of salt, Gandhi organised a march to the sea in Dandi, over 241 miles away, to make his own salt. Around 60,000 people were arrested and the police beat many people.

After many years of protesting and acts of civil disobedience, Britain eventually gave India independence in 1947. Sadly, Gandhi was shot and killed in 1948 and never saw India's official day of independence. However, he will be remembered as leader of the Indian independence movement who fought for freedom and equality via peaceful protests.

TIMELINE: MEN WHO CHANGED THE WORLD

1452: Leonardo da Vinci is born in Vinci, Italy.

1564: William Shakespeare is born in Stratford-Upon-Avon, England.

1687: Sir Isaac Newton publishes his theory of gravity.

1752: Benjamin Franklin conducts his famous kite experiment and discovers electricity.

1989: Sir Tim Berners-Lee invents the World Wide Web.

1963: Martin Luther King leads a 250,000 strong march on Washington to fight for civil rights and an end to segregation.

1948: India gains independence from Britain afters years of non-violent protests organised by Mahatma Gandhi.

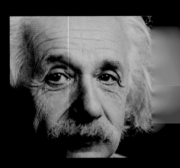

1905: Albert Einstein publishes his theory of relativity.

1994: Nelson Mandela becomes the president of South Africa.

2009: Barack Obama officially becomes the first African-American president and the 44th president of the United States.

MORE MEN WHO CHANGED THE WORLD

Abraham Lincoln – American president who helped end slavery.

Charles Darwin – Discovered evolution and the theory of natural selection.

Galileo Galilei – Italian astronomer, scientist and philosopher who made many scientific advances and discoveries.

Louis Pasteur – Scientist who developed many cures and learned how to make milk safe to drink.

Edward Jenner – Invented vaccines (medicines which prevent someone getting a certain disease).

Mozart – Famous musician who wrote many symphonies.

There are lots more men who, throughout history, have made big decisions, invented or discovered important things, and campaigned for change. Without them, the world would not be the same. Who else can you think of? Which men have made the biggest impact on your world?

GLOSSARY

abolished
to have put an end to something, usually a system, practice or institution

African National Congress
a political party in South Africa who wanted to end apartheid

amateur
someone who engages in sport for pleasure rather than to be a professional

astronomer
a person who studies the universe and objects in space

atom
the smallest possible piece of anything

boycott
to stop using the goods or services of a certain company or country as a means of protest

British Empire
a term previously used to describe all of the territories controlled by Britain

carpentry
the work of a carpenter

civil disobedience
the refusal to follow certain laws or demands set by the government

civil rights activist
a person who is part of a political movement to secure equal opportunities and rights

Civil Rights Movement
a movement in 1950s and 1960s America that fought for racial equality and an end to segregation

commemorate
to remember officially or give respect to someone or something, especially by making a statue or building

conductor
a material that allows heat or electricity to go through it

democratic
relating to political or social equality

discriminated
to have treated people unjustly for reasons, such as their race, gender, sex or age

dismantled
to have pulled down or taken apart

feats
achievements that are difficult to make

government
a group of people with the authority to run a country and decide its laws

legacy
things that you pass on

mass
the amount of matter that a body or object contains

orbited
when an object has made a path around a larger object in space

president
the person who runs a country

racial equality
the state of being equal in terms of race

segregation
the act of separating or setting apart people based on race

senate
an assembly of politicians who help to create laws

sonnets
poems that have particular forms and are usually about love

static electricity
electricity that can be created by friction

virtual
existing only online

INDEX

A

African National Congress 10-11

art 14-15

B

Berners-Lee, Sir Timothy 5, 22-23, 28

boxing 18-19

British Empire,the 26

C

civil rights 5-7, 10, 26, 28

Clay, Cassius 18

D

da Vinci, Leonardo 5, 14-15, 28

democracy 11

discrimination 7, 26

drawings 14-15

E

Earth, the 9

Einstein, Albert 5, 20-21, 28

electricity 4, 12-13, 28

equality 4, 6-7, 10-11, 16-17, 19, 27

F

Franklin, Benjamin 5, 12-13, 28

G

Gandhi, Mahatma 5, 26-28

Globe Theatre, the 25

governments 10, 27

gravity 5, 8-9, 21

I

India 5, 26-27

Internet, the 5, 23

inventions 4, 21, 23

K

King, Martin Luther 5-7, 28

L

law 16, 26

– apartheid 10-11

– Obamacare 17

– segregation 6

light 12-13, 20-21

M

Mandela, Nelson 5, 10-11, 28

Mona Lisa 14

N

Newton, Sir Isaac 5, 8-9, 28

O

Obama, Barack 5, 16-17

P

paintings 14-15

Parks, Rosa 6

physics 20-21

plays 5, 24-25

politics 4, 16-17

presidents 4-5, 11, 16-17, 19

protests 6-7, 27

R

relativity 5, 20

Renaissance, the 14

S

scientists 4, 8, 12, 15, 21

Shakespeare, William 5, 24-25

sonnets 24

South Africa 5, 10-11, 26

sports 5, 18-19

U

USA 6, 16, 18

V

voting 11, 16, 19

W

World Wide Web 22